KETO CHAFFLE RECIPE COOBOOK 2021

Simple and Delicious Low-Carb Recipes with Pictures to Lose Weight and Bost Metabolism

ANDYNA COOK

DISCLAIMER

TABLE OF CONTENT

Introduction

Chaffles are made using cheese and eggs. Cheese+ waffles make chaffles. Crazy as they sound, they're amazingly easy to make. Eggs and cheese are the principal ingredients, and they hold together shockingly well on a waffle iron. Use them as a treat, or have them for two or three times each week. All things considered, there's nothing in the recipes you can't eat on a low-carb diet. These are a wonderful method to feel like you're having a treat without going astray from your eating regimen by any means. Without a doubt, they might be savory whereas ordinary waffles are sweet, and they may not combine well with maple syrup. Yet, this is as yet significant on the grounds that one of the factors that decide diet achievement is the number of food alternatives you have accessible to you. These special and innovative food sources have begun as a pattern among those after prohibitive diets. Chaffles contain no flour, which means they are on low carb keto diet. They have become so main stream that even the individuals who aren't on the keto diet need to attempt them as well. They contain cheese which has the ideal macronutrient structure in case you're on a low-carb diet. It's loaded with muscle-building proteins and satisfying fats, and has for all intents and purposes no carbs. Cheese is produced using whey protein, perhaps the best sort of protein you can eat after an exercise to help fix muscle tissue. What's more, one egg likewise contains in excess of 6 grams of protein, making these the most protein-pressed waffles you're truly going to eat. Also, in case you're attempting to remain low-carb on a careful spending plan, they're the most reasonable protein source you will discover. You can eat them as sweet treats, as a morning meal supper or as a bite. Chaffles are alive and well food varieties that follow the ketogenic diet suggestions. They are high-fat, high-protein, and low-starch food sources that can tell the body the best way to utilize fat as an elective fuel to create energy and consume fat.

In this book I will examine chaffles and clarify how they are unique in relation to waffles. I'll clarify the various sorts of chaffles you can undoubtedly make at home. I will likewise dive deep into the ketogenic count calories and talk about its numerous advantages.

These are the things that you will discover in this book

- Health advantages of the ketogenic diet
- Carb count and chaffle nutrition
- Most delicious chaffle recipes

At long last, I will likewise be sharing numerous delectable Keto Chaffle recipes that are altogether simple to get ready. For every recipe, I will give a rundown of ingredients and point by point bit by bit instructions. I'm sure you will discover this book extremely valuable. Enjoy reading delicious recipes!

What Is Ketogenic Diet and
Its Benefits

The keto or ketogenic diet recommends eating high-fat, low-carb foods that provide us with healthy fats, proteins, and fewer carbohydrates. The calories we consume come mainly from fats (70%), proteins (20%) and carbohydrates (10%). The diet usually does not count calories. Carbohydrates are counted and limited instead.

The human body converts carbohydrates into glucose to produce energy. Fats, which can also be used to make energy, are largely ignored, which is why it is deposited and we are chased. The ketogenic diet limits carbohydrate intake and stimulates the body to burn fat for energy. For this reason, the ketogenic diet is considered to be very efficient for weight loss.

Even if you eat fewer carbohydrates, the insulin level in the abdomen goes down, so that there is less glucose.

Ketogenic Diet Health Benefits

Not just weight loss, the keto diet helps us in many ways -

- Blood Sugar - It can help us lower blood sugar and insulin levels. A low-carbohydrate diet also prevents spikes in blood sugar.

- Cholesterol - It increases the level of healthy HDL cholesterol and lowers the unhealthy LDL cholesterol. So, it reduces the risk of heart disease.

- The Human Brain - Studies have shown that low-carb, high-protein, and fatty foods make our brains more efficient. It can prevent or slow down Alzheimer's disease, dementia, autism and other similar cognitive diseases.

- Inflammation - Inflammation improves immunity, but chronic inflammation can cause health problems. The keto diet decreases free radical production and controls the negative effects of too much inflammation such as arthritis, eczema and psoriasis.

- Stomach Health - A low-carb diet provides relief from heartburn and acid reflux. It can combat the main problems such as bacterial problems and autoimmune reactions. It also improves digestion.

- Anti-aging - According to research results, the ketogenic diet can also promote longevity.

- Improves Energy - The diet stabilizes insulin levels and provides more energy to the brain and tissues. It also improves slow sleep patterns and decreases REM (Rapid Eye Movement) or superficial sleep.

- PCOS - Carbohydrate-rich foods are not recommended for people suffering from PCOS or polycystic ovary syndrome. Studies have shown that keto foods can improve PCOS markers.

- Triglycerides - Triglyceride levels in the blood can skyrocket if we consume too many carbohydrates, leading to an increased risk of heart disease. Reduce consumption and there is a drastic drop in the level.

Apart from the ones mentioned above, the ketogenic diet can also help us control uric acid levels, improve the health of our eyes, and prevent acne breakouts.

Foods that are allowed and not allowed in the keto diet

What you can eat -

1. Seafood, including sardines, salmon, shrimp, crabs, and tuna. Fatty fish such as sardines and salmon are particularly good.

2. Fresh leafy greens, including broccoli, kale, spinach, cauliflower, turnips, cucumber, lettuce, asparagus, bell pepper.

3. Dairy products, including yogurt and cheese. Avoid flavored yogurt.

4. Meat, including pork, lamb, beef, chicken, and turkey, is allowed.

5. Eggs are rich in protein and are allowed in the keto diet.

6. You can eat nuts and seeds in moderation. Avoid cashews.

7. Tea and coffee are both allowed, but without sugar.

8. Use coconut oil for frying and sautéing.

9. You can have dark chocolate with 80% cocoa.

Foods to avoid -

1. Limit the intake of fruits because most of them contain too much sugar.

2. Most grains are high in sugar and are best avoided.

3. White starches only add empty calories.

4. Beans and legumes are high in carbohydrates.

5. Limit the intake of alcohol and honey.

Breakfast Chaffle Recipes

Cheesy Jalapeño Chaffles

Servings: 1 Cook time: 5 min

INGREDIENTS

- 1/3 cup shredded cheese, divided
- 1 egg
- 1 tablespoon almond flour
- 1-2 tablespoons chopped jalapeño

TRAVEL DIRECTIONS

1. Preheat your waffle maker. When hot, spray with a tiny amount of nonstick cooking spray.
2. While the waffle maker is heating, whisk together 2/3 of the cheese, egg, almond flour and jalapeño in a bowl.

3. Add a small pinch of the remaining cheese to the waffle maker (this helps make a crispy chaffle), add 1/2 of the batter, top with another tiny pinch of cheese (for crispy top), close, and when the light goes off, it's ready (about 3 to 4 minutes).
4. Remove the chaffle from waffle maker and place on paper towel to soak up any extra oil. Repeat with remaining to make a second chaffle.

Nutritional Information:

- 200 calories, 13 grams fat, 2.5 net carbs and 15 grams protein

Cinnamon Roll Chaffle

Servings: 2 Cook time: 5 min

INGREDIENTS

- 2 eggs
- 3 tablespoons ZenSweet Monk Fruit Sweetener
- 2 tablespoons almond flour
- 1/2 teaspoon cinnamon
- 1/2 teaspoon baking soda
- 1/4 teaspoon sea salt
- 1 cup mozzarella cheese shredded
- cooking spray avocado or coconut oil
- 2 ounces cream cheese
- 3 tablespoons heavy whipping cream
- 1 tablespoon Monk Fruit Sweetener

TRAVEL DIRECTIONS

1. Firstly add eggs to a medium sized mixing bowl, and whisk to mix .
   Then Add the sweetener almond flour, cinnamon, baking soda, sea salt,

and vanilla, and whisk again. Add the mozzarella cheese and mix to coat in the egg batter.

2. Spray a waffle iron along with coconut oil or avocado oil, and cook it. Once it's preheated, add some of the chaffle batter to the center of your waffle iron, being careful not to overfill it. The batter will spread and rise as it cooks. Heat the chaffle for about 4-5 minutes, until it has browned and the waffle iron stops steaming.

3. Then Top the chaffles with the glaze, and strawberries or sugar free maple syrup, if desired.

Nutritional Information:

- 448kcalories

Keto Chaffle with Scallion Cream Cheese

Serving: 1 Cook time: 4-5 min

INGREDIENTS

- 1 Large Egg
- 1/2 Cup of Shredded Mozzarella
- 2 Tbsp of Cream Cheese
- 1 Tbsp of Bagel Seasoning
- 1-2 Scallions (Green Onions), Sliced

TRAVEL DIRECTIONS

1. Firstly, preheat the Mini Waffle 'Chaffle' maker.
2. Crack the egg into a small bowl and mix with 1/2 cup of shredded mozzarella. This paste will make 2 Chaffles.
3. Now Pour 1/2 the mix into the pre-heated Chaffle maker and allow to cook for 3-4 minutes (depending on how crispy you prefer your Chaffles)
4. Remove the Chaffle and repeat by pouring the other half of the mix into your Chaffle maker and cooking for 3-4 minutes.
5. Allow chaffles to cool then spread cream cheese on each, scatter generously with Bagel seasoning and add your sliced scallions.

Nutritional Information:

- Per serving: 200 calories, 13 grams fat, 2.5 net carbs and 15 grams protein

Chaffle Breakfast Sandwich

Servings: 1 Cooking time: 5 min

INGREDIENTS

- 1 tablespoon butter
- 1 fried egg
- 1 sausage patty, cooked

TRAVEL DIRECTIONS

1. Firstly Preheat waffle maker and combine all the maple chaffle

INGREDIENTS in a small bowl.

2. Then Pour 1/2 the batter into the waffle maker and cook until set - about 3 to 5 minutes.
3. Then remove the maple waffle once finished cooking. Repeat with remaining batter.
4. Spread butter on one side of each maple chaffle. Top with fried egg and heated sausage patty.

Nutritional Information:

- 685 Calories, 54.5g Fat, 36.6g Protein 5.2g

Keto Sausage Ball Chaffles

Servings: 12 Cook time: 4 min

INGREDIENTS

- 1 lb ground sausage
- ⅓ cup coconut flour
- 1 cup shredded cheddar cheese
- 2 eggs
- 2 tsp baking powder
- Sugar Free Maple Syrup

TRAVEL DIRECTIONS

1. Firstly Preheat waffle maker.
2. Then Mix all together in a large bowl until mixed together.
3. Using a cookie scoop or large spoon, scoop about 3-4 tablespoons of sausage mixture into the waffle maker. Close it and cook for about 4 minutes.
4. Repeat with remaining paste.
5. Serve sausage chaffles.

Nutritional Information:

- Per Servings: Protein: 45% 140 kcal fat: 51% 160 kcal carbohydrates: 4% 14 kcal

Egg on A Cheddar Cheese Chaffle

Servings: 4 Cooking time: 7-9 minutes

INGREDIENTS
- Seizure
- 4 eggs
- 2 cups of shredded white cheddar cheese
- Salt and pepper to taste
- Others
- 2 tablespoons of butter for brushing the waffle iron
- 4 large eggs
- 2 tablespoons of olive oil

TRAVEL *DIRECTIONS*
1. Preheat the waffle iron.
2. Crack the eggs into a bowl and beat with a fork.
3. Stir in the grated cheddar cheese and season with salt and pepper.
4. Brush the heated waffle iron with butter and add a few tablespoons of the batter.
5. Close the lid and cook for about 7-8 minutes, depending on your waffle iron.
6. Cook the eggs while chaffles are cooking.
7. Heat the oil in a large non-stick pan with lid over medium heat for 2-3 minutes

8. Break an egg into a small bowl and carefully put it in the pan. Repeat the same way for the other 3 eggs.

9. Cover and cook for 2 to 2 ½ minutes for textured eggs but with runny yolks.

10. Remove from heat.

11. Before serving, place a chaffle on each plate and top with an egg. Season with salt and black pepper.

Nutritional Information:

- *Per Servings:* Calories 4, Fat 34g, Carbohydrates 2g, Sugar 0.6g, Protein 26g, Sodium 518mg

Keto Blueberry Chaffle Recipe

Servings: 5 Cook Time: 15 min

INGREDIENTS

- 1 cup shredded mozzarella cheese
- 2 tbsp almond flour
- 3 tbsp blueberries
- 1 tsp cinnamon
- 2 tsp Swerve
- 2 eggs

TRAVEL DIRECTIONS

1. Firstly, heat waffle maker.
2. Then In a bowl, mix all **INGREDIENTS** and combine well.
3. Using a non-stick spray, coat waffle maker before putting batter inside.
4. The batter will make 4 mini chaffles, you can use an ice cream scoop for measurement or about ¼ cup. Just make sure not to overfill the waffle maker.

Nutritional Information:

- Per serving: Calories: 115 Net Carbs: 3

Coconut Chaffles

Servings: 2 Cooking time: 5 minutes

INGREDIENTS

- 1 egg
- 1 oz. cream cheese,
- 1 oz. cheddar cheese
- 2 tablespoons. coconut flour
- 1 tsp. stevia
- 1 tbsp. coconut oil, melted
- 1/2 tsp. coconut extract
- 2 eggs, simmer before serving

TRAVEL *DIRECTIONS*

1. Heat your Minute i Dash waffle iron and grease with cooking spray.
2. Mix all Chaffles in a bowl.
3. Pour the whipped cream batter into a preheated waffle iron.
4. Close the lid.
5. Cook chaffles for about 2-3 minutes until golden brown.
6. Serve with a boiled egg and enjoy!

Nutritional Information:

- Per Servings: Protein: 21% 32 kcal Fat:% 117 kcal Carbohydrates: 3% 4 kcal

Garlic and Parsley Chaffles

Servings: 1 Cooking time: 5 minutes

INGREDIENTS

- 1 large egg
- 1/4 cup of cheese mozzarella
- 1 tsp. coconut flour
- ¼ tsp. baking powder
- ½ tsp. garli c powder
- 1 tbsp. finely chopped parsley
- To serve
- Poach egg
- 4 oz. smoked salmon

TRAVEL DIRECTIONS

1. Turn on your Dash Minute Waffle Iron and let it preheat.
2. Grease the waffle iron with cooking spray.
3. Combine egg, mozzarella, coconut flour, baking powder and garlic powder, parsley in a mixing bowl until well combined.
4. Pour the batter into the circle hook.
5. Close the lid.
6. Cook for about 2-3 minutes or until the chaffles are tender.
7. Serve with smoked salmon and poached egg.
8. To enjoy!

Nutritional Information:

- Per Servings: Protein: 45% 140 kcal fat: 51% 160 kcal carbohydrates: 4% 14 kcal

Chaffle Cake & Sandwich Recipes

Strawberry Cream Sandwich Chaffles

Servings: 2 Cooking time: 6 minutes

INGREDIENTS

- Chaffles
- 1 large organic egg, beaten
- ½ cup of mozzarella cheese, finely chopped
- Stuffing
- 4 teaspoons of whipped cream
- 2 tablespoons of erythritol powder
- 1 teaspoon of fresh lemon juice
- Pinch of fresh lemon zest, grated
- 2 fresh strawberries, peeled and sliced

TRAVEL DIRECTIONS

1. Preheat a mini waffle iron and then grease it.
2. For chaffles: In a small bowl, add the egg and mozzarella cheese and stir to combine.

3. Place half of the mixture in the preheated waffle iron and cook for about 2 minutes.

4. Repeat with the remaining mixture.
5. Meanwhile for filling: In a bowl, put all except the strawberry slices and beat with a hand mixer until well blended.
6. Serve each chaffle with the cream mixture and strawberry slices.

Nutritional information:

- Calories 95 Net carbohydrates 1.4 g Total fat 5 g Saturated fat 3.9 g Cholesterol 110 mg Sodium 82 mg Total carbohydrates 1.7 g Fiber 0.3 g Sugar 0.9 g Protein 5.5 g

Ham Sandwich Chaffles

Servings: 2 Cooking time: 8 minutes

INGREDIENTS

- 1 organic egg, beaten
- ½ cup of Monterrey Jack cheese, shredded
- 1 teaspoon of coconut flour
- Pinch of garlic powder
- Stuffing
- 2 sugar-free slices of ham
- 1 small tomato, sliced
- 2 salad leaves

TRAVEL DIRECTIONS

1. Preheat a mini waffle iron and then grease it.
2. For chaffles: put all in a medium bowl and mix with a fork until well blended. Place half of the mixture in the preheated waffle iron and cook for about 3-4 minutes.
3. Repeat with the remaining mixture.

4. Serve each chaffle with filling.

Nutritional information:
- Calories 1 Net carbohydrates 3.7 g Total fat 8.7 g Saturated fat 3.4 g Cholesterol 114 mg Sodium 794 mg Total carbohydrates 5.5 g Fiber 1.8 g Sugar 1.5 g Protein 13.9 g

Chicken Sandwich Chaffles

Servings: 2 Cooking time: 8 minutes

INGREDIENTS

- Chaffles
- 1 large organic egg, beaten
- ½ cup of cheddar cheese, shredded
- Pinch of salt and ground black pepper
- Stuffing
- 1 (6-ounce) cooked chicken breast, halved
- 2 salad leaves
- ¼ small onion, sliced
- 1 small tomato, sliced

TRAVEL DIRECTIONS

1. Preheat a mini waffle iron and then grease it.

2. For chaffles: put all in a medium bowl and mix with a fork until well blended. Place half of the mixture in the preheated waffle iron and cook for about 3-4 minutes.
3. Repeat with the remaining mixture.
4. Serve each chaffle with filling

Nutritional information:
- Calories 2 Net carbohydrates 2.5 g Total fat 14.1 g Saturated fat 6.8 g Cholesterol 177 mg Sodium 334 mg Total carbohydrates 3.3 g Fiber 0.8 g Sugar 2 g Protein 28.7 g

Salmon & Cheese Sandwich Chaffles

Servings: 4 Cooking time: 24 minutes

INGREDIENTS:

- Chaffles
- 2 organic eggs
- ½ ounce butter, melted
- 1 cup mozzarella cheese, shredded
- 2 tablespoons of almond flour
- Pinch of salt
- Stuffing
- ½ cup of smoked salmon
- 1/3 cup avocado, peeled, pitted, and sliced
- 2 tablespoons feta cheese, crumbled

TRAVEL DIRECTIONS

1. Preheat a mini waffle iron and then grease it.
2. For chaffles: put all in a medium bowl and mix with a fork until well blended. Place 1/4 of the mixture in preheated waffle iron and cook for about 5-6 minutes.
3. Repeat with the remaining mixture.
4. Serve each chaffle with filling.

Nutritional information:

- Calories 169 Net carbohydrates 1.2 g Total fat 13 g Saturated fat 5 g Cholesterol 101 mg Sodium 319 mg Total carbohydrates 2.8 g Fiber 1.6 g Sugar 0.6 g Protein 8.9 g

Strawberry Cream Cheese Sandwich Chaffles

Servings: 2 Cooking time: 10 minutes

INGREDIENTS

- Chaffle s
- 1 organic egg, beaten
- 1 teaspoon of organic vanilla extract
- 1 tablespoon of almond flour
- 1 teaspoon of organic baking powder
- Pinch of ground cinnamon
- 1 cup mozzarella cheese, shredded
- Stuffing
- 2 tablespoons cream cheese, softened
- 2 tablespoons of erythritol
- ¼ teaspoon of organic vanilla extract
- 2 fresh strawberries, peeled and cut into pieces

TRAVEL DIRECTIONS

1. Preheat a mini waffle iron and then grease it.

2. For chaffles: in a bowl add the egg and vanilla extract and mix well.

3. Add the flour, baking powder and cinnamon and mix until well blended.

4. Add the mozzarella cheese and stir to combine.

5. Put half of the mixture in the preheated waffle iron and cook for about 4 minutes.

6. Repeat with the remaining mixture.

7. Meanwhile, for filling: in a bowl, put all the except the strawberry pieces and beat with a hand mixer until well blended.

8. Serve each chaffle with a cream cheese mixture and strawberry pieces.

Nutritional information:

- calories 143 Net carbohydrates: g Total fat 10.1 g Saturated fat 4.5 g Cholesterol 100 mg Sodium 1 48 mg Total carbohydrates 4.1 g Fiber 0.8 g Sugar 1.2 g Protein 7.6 g

Egg & Bacon Sandwich Chaffles

Servings: 4 Cooking time: 20 minutes

INGREDIENTS

- Chaffles
- 2 large organic eggs, beaten
- 4 tablespoons of almond flour
- 1 teaspoon of organic baking powder
- 1 cup mozzarella cheese, shredded
- Stuffing
- 4 organic fried eggs
- 4 cooked slices of bacon

TRAVEL DIRECTIONS

1. Preheat a mini waffle iron and then grease it.
2. Place all in a medium bowl and mix with a fork until well blended. Place half of the mixture in a preheated waffle iron and cook for about 3-5 minutes.
3. Repeat with the remaining mixture.
4. Repeat with the remaining mixture.
5. Serve each chaffle with filling

Nutritional information:

- Calories 197 Net carbohydrates: g Total fat 14.5 g Saturated fat 4.1 g Cholesterol 2 mg Sodium 224 g Total carbohydrates 2.7 g Fiber 0.8 g Sugar 0.8 g Protein 12.9 g

Blueberries Peanut Butter Sandwich Chaffles

Servings: 2 Cooking time: 10 minutes

INGREDIENTS

- 1 organic egg, beaten
- ½ cup of cheddar cheese, shredded
- Stuffing
- 2 tablespoons of erythritol
- 1 tablespoon butter, softened
- 1 tablespoon of natural peanut butter
- 2 tablespoons cream cheese, softened
- ¼ teaspoon of organic vanilla extract
- 2 teaspoons of fresh blueberries

TRAVEL DIRECTIONS

1. Preheat a mini waffle iron and then grease it.
2. For chaffles: In a small bowl, add the egg and cheddar cheese and stir to combine.
3. Put half of the mixture in the preheated waffle iron and cook for about 5 minutes.
4. Repeat with the remaining mixture.
5. Meanwhile for filling: put all in a medium bowl and mix until well blended.

6. Serve each chaffle with a peanut butter mixture.

Nutritional information:
Calories 143 Net carbohydrates 3.3 g Total fat 10.1 g Saturated fat 4.5 g Cholesterol 100 mg Sodium 148 mg Total carbohydrates 4.1 g Fiber 0.8 g Sugar 1.2 g Protein 6 g

Festive Chaffle Recipes

Spooky Keto Chocolate Chaffles

Serving: 5-6 Cook time: 50 min

INGREDIENTS

- large egg

- 1 large egg white

- tbsp cream cheese (30 g/ 1.1 oz)

- 1/2 cup grated mozzarella (57 g/ 2 oz)

- cup full-fat cream cheese (60 g/ 2.1 oz)

- 1/4 tsp sugar-free vanilla extract

TRAVEL DIRECTIONS

1. Firstly, preheat the mini waffle maker. Prepare all of the for the chaffle

   batter. Start with the whole egg, egg white, mozzarella and cream cheese and bend until smooth. Add the dry (cocoa powder, coconut flour and baking powder) and blend again until well combined.

2. Then Cook each waffle (about 50 g/1.8 oz batter) in a preheated mini waffle maker for 2 to 3 minutes.

3. Then Open the waffle maker and let the chaffle rest to cool down slightly. Open the waffle maker, let the chaffle cool down for 15 seconds, and then use a spatula to remove and let cool down completely. Repeat this until you make 5 chaffles. Meanwhile, while the chaffles are cooling down, place the whipping cream, cream cheese, vanilla extract and powdered Erythritol in the bowl of a mixer. Using the whisker whisk until thick and creamy.

4. Place the mixture in a piping bag and decorate in any way you like. I tried to draw a spooky skeleton face but you can just spread the paste on top using a spoon. The mixture is thick so you may need to use a spoon to smoothen your decorations Store the separate components in the fridge for up to 3 days and decorate on the day you plan to serve them. For longer storage, freeze the chaffles for up to 3 months.

Nutritional Information: Calories

- Eggs, free-range or organic
- 0.1 g 1.3 g 1 g   14 kcal

Keto Peanut Butter Cup Chaffle

Serving: 1 Cook time: 10 min

INGREDIENTS:

- Egg
- tbsp Heavy Cream
- tbsp Unsweetened Cocoa
- tbsp Powdered Sweetener
- tsp Coconut Flour
- 1/2 tsp Vanilla Extract
- Heavy cream

TRAVEL DIRECTIONS

1. First of all, preheat mini waffle maker.

2. Then pour half of the chaffle mixture into the center of the waffle iron. Allow to cook for 3-5 minutres.

3. Then Carefully remove and repeat for second chaffle. Allow chaffles to sit for a few minutes so that they crisp up.

4. For peanut butter filling, blend all ingredients together and spread between chaffles.

Nutritional Information:

- YIELD: 2 Chaffles SERVING SIZE: 1, including the filling
- Amount Per Serving: CALORIES: 264 TOTAL FAT: 21.6g CARBOHYDRATES: 7.25g NET CARBOHYDRATES: 4.5g FIBER: 2.75g PROTEIN: 9.45g

Maple Pecan Keto Chaffles

Serving: 2 Cook time: 5 minutes

INGREDIENTS

- large egg
- 1/2 cup mozzarella cheese finely shredded
- 1/4 cup almond flour
- tablespoon pecans
- tablespoon brown allulose

TRAVEL DIRECTIONS

1. Firstly, preheat a mini-waffle maker. Put egg in a small combine bowl and lightly whisk.

2. Then spray waffle iron with coconut oil. Scoop half of the batter onto the waffle iron, close the iron.

Ranch Blt Chaffles Sandwich

Serving: 2 Cook time: 35 min

INGREDIENTS

- 2 eggs

- 2 leaves of lettuce

- 2 slices of tomato

- 4 slices bacon, cooked

- Ranch dressing or Mayo is optional

- Mini Waffle Iron

- Cheese

TRAVEL DIRECTIONS

1. First mix both cheeses and the eggs into a bowl.

2. Then ranch seasoning and whisk everything together.

3. Plug the Mini Waffle Iron and let it warm up.

4. Once becomes ready, spoon 2 -3 spoon fulls of mixture into mini waffle iron.

Nutrition Information:

- Serving: 1g | Calories: 151kcal | Carbohydrates: 5g | Protein: 6g | Fat: 13g | Saturated Fat: 6g | Cholesterol: 111mg | Sodium: 83mg | Potassium: 190mg | Fiber: 2g | Sugar: 1g | Vitamin A: 461IU | Calcium: 67mg | Iron: 1mg

Keto Chocolate Waffles | Eeasy & Flourless

Serving: 3 Cook time: 10 min

INGREDIENTS

- large Egg

- 33 grams Kite Hill Almond Cream Cheese,

- 1/8 tsp Pure Monk Fruit Extract

- 1/8 tsp Almond Flavor

- 1 Tbsp Virgin Coconut Oil

TRAVEL DIRECTIONS

1. Firstly melt coconut oil and add to your cream cheese.

2. Combine coconut oil and cream cheese together.

3. Beat big egg in a separate bowl.

4. Combine everything together. Pour paste into your waffle maker for about 4-5 minutes or until steam stops.

Easy Pumpkin Chocolate Chip Chaffles

Serving: 3 Cook time: 20 min

INGREDIENTS

- 1/2 cup shredded mozzarella cheese

- 4 teaspoons pumpkin puree

- 1 egg

- 2 tablespoons swerve

- 1/4 tsp pumpkin spice

- 4 teaspoons sugar free chocolate chips

- 1 tablespoon almond flour

TRAVEL DIRECTIONS

1.   Plug in your waffle maker.

2.   In a small bowl mix the pumpkin puree and egg. Make sure you mix it well so all the pumpkin is mixed with the egg.

3. Next add in the mozzarella cheese, almond flour, swerve and pumpkin spice and mix well.

4. Then add in your sugar free chocolate chips and add half the keto pumpkin pie Chaffle mix to the Dish Mini waffle maker at a time. Cook chaffle batter in the waffle maker for 4 minutes.

5. When the first one is completely done cooking cook the second one.

6. Presenter with some swerve confectioner's sweetener or whipped cream on top.

Nutrition

- Serving: 1g | Calories: 93kcal | Carbohydrates: 2g | Protein: 7g | Fat: 7g | Saturated

   Fat: 3g | Cholesterol: 69mg | Sodium: 138mg | Potassium: 48mg | Fiber: 1g | Sugar: 1g | Vitamin A: 1228IU | Calcium: 107mg | Iron: 1mg

Keto Chaffle Chocolate Glaze Donut

Serving: 6 Cook time: 10 min

INGREDIENTS

For the chaffle:

- ½ cup Mozzarella cheddar shredded

- ounce Cream cheddar

- tablespoon Almond flour

- tablespoon Swerve confectioners sugar substitute

- ½ teaspoon Baking powder

- ½ teaspoon Vanilla concentrate

- 1 Eggs

- For the chocolate coat:

- tablespoon Lily's heating chips

Meat chaffle Recipes

Dinner Salmon Chaffle Tacos

Servings: 4 Cook time: 10 min

INGREDIENTS

- 26 oz jars of salmon

- cup almond flour

- eggs

- 1 jalapeño (diced)

- ½ red onion (diced)

- ½ cup green onion (diced)

- 1 orange pepper (diced)

- 1 tsp minced garlic

- 1 tsp dill

- 1 lemon (squeezed)

- tbsp mayo

- 1 cup matchstick carrots

- 1 tbsp Siracha Mayo

- 1 tbsp Greek yogurt

- Margarine lettuce

TRAVEL DIRECTIONS

1. Dice vegetables, channel salmon (eliminate bones if material)

2. Add salmon, almond flour, eggs, salt, jalapeño, red onion, garlic, mayo, lemon juice, dill, pepper, and a large portion of the green onion a bowl and blend well

3. Preheat waffle iron

4. Structure 4-5 patties (contingent upon the size of the waffle iron)

5. Cook in waffle iron 3-4 minutes each

6. Cut into strips

7. Spot a touch of matchstick carrots onto spread lettuce "tortilla"

8. Put salmon chaffle strip in the focal point of margarine lettuce on top of carrots and top with staying green onion, Greek yogurt, and sriracha mayo.

Nutritional Information:

- Amount Per Serving: CALORIES: 494 TOTAL FAT: 35g SATURATED FAT: 5g TRANS FAT: 0g UNSATURATED FAT: 28g CHOLESTEROL: 151mg SODIUM: 868mg CARBOHYDRATES: 18g FIBER: 7g SUGAR: 7g PROTEIN: 30g

Mexiketo Chipotle Beef Chaffle Tacos

Serving: 4 Cook time: 10 min Chaffles

INGREDIENTS

- 2 cup shredded (cheddar or mozzarella)

- 2 eggs

- 1/2 tsp Italian flavoring

- 1/4 tsp salt

- Taco Meat

- 1lb ground hamburger

- 1 tsp bean stew powder

- 1 tsp ground cumin

- 1/3 teaspoon garlic powder

- 1/2 teaspoon cocoa powder

- 1/4 teaspoon onion powder

- 1/4 teaspoon salt

- 1/12 tsp smoked paprika

- 1⁄2 cup Cholula Chipotle Hot Sauce™
- Taco Toppings
- 3⁄4 cup pico de gallo
- 1⁄2 cup guacamole
- 1⁄2 cup harsh cream
- 1 cup shredded lettuce
- chopped scallions

TRAVEL DIRECTIONS;

1. Cook ground hamburger in an enormous skillet until brown over medium heat.

2. Include bean stew powder, cumin, garlic, cocoa powder, onion powder, paprika, salt, and Cholula Chipotle Hot Sauce. Lessen heat and permit to stew for 5—6 minutes.

3. While the meat is stewing, preheat your waffle producer.

4. Whip eggs in a little bowl. Include shredded cheddar, salt, and flavors.

5. Gap chaffle combination into 4 even segments, and cook each part on the pre-heated waffle producer to make your shells. Each chaffle should cook for 3—4 minutes.

6. Fill you chaffles with the taco meat.

7. Top it with lettuce, guacamole, pico de gallo, acrid cream, or whatever your #1 taco garnishes are. Shower wanted measure of Cholula Chipotle Hot Sauce on top for additional flavor, lastly embellish.

Nutritional Information:

- Calories 4, Fat 35.8g, Carbohydrates 3.3g, Sugar 0.8g, Protein 40.3g, Sodium 200mg

Chaffle easy Meat Recipe

Serving: 1 Cook time: 10 minutes

INGREDIENTS

For the hamburger:

- 1/2 cup hamburger stock

- 4 ounces meager cut shop cook meat

- For the chaffle bun:

- egg, beaten

- 1 teaspoon coconut flour

- 1/4 teaspoon preparing powder

- 1/2 cup finely shredded mozzarella

- For the low carb Arby's sauce:

- 1 tablespoon without sugar ketchup

- teaspoons Italian serving of mixed greens dressing

- 1/4 teaspoon Worcestershire sauce

- 1/4 teaspoon broke pepper

TRAVEL DIRECTIONS

For the meat:

1. Add the hamburger stock to a skillet and bring to a stew. Add the hamburger and cook on low for 5 minutes to warm meat through. Cover and put in a safe spot while setting up the chaffle.

For the chaffle:

1. Plug in the waffle iron to preheat.

2. Whisk together the egg, coconut flour, and heating powder. Mix in the mozzarella to join.

3. Spoon half of the player into the waffle iron. Close the waffle creator and cook for 3 minutes. Eliminate the waffle and rehash with residual player.

4. For the Arby's sauce:

ARBY'S roast Chaffles

Servings: 2 Cooking time: 11 minutes

INGREDIENTS

- 1 /2 cup grated Mozzarella
- 1 egg
- 1/2 teaspoon of basil
- 1/4 teaspoon of garlic powder
- 1 tbsp almond flour
- 1 tbsp butter
- 1/4 teaspoon of garlic powder
- 1/4 cup of grated mozzarella cheese

TRAVEL DIRECTIONS

1. Heat your Dash mini waffle iron.
2. In a small bowl, combine the egg, 1/2 teaspoon of basil, 1/4 teaspoon of garlic powder, 1 tablespoon of almond flour, and 1/2 cup of mozzarella cheese.
3. Add 1/2 of the batter to your mini waffle iron and cook for 4 minutes. If they are still a little uncooked, let it cook for 2 more minutes. Then boil the rest of the batter to make a second chaffle.
4. In a small bowl, add 1 tablespoon of butter and 1 / teaspoon of garlic powder and melt in the microwave. It takes about 25 seconds, depending on your microwave.

5. Chaffles Lay on a baking sheet and divide with a rubber brush the butter and garlic mixture over it.

6. Add 1 / 8th cup of cheese to each chaffle.

7. Place chaffles in the oven or a toaster oven at 400 degrees and cook until the cheese has melted.

Nutritional Information:

- Calories: 231 kcal; Carbohydrates: 2 g; Protein: 13 g; Fat: 19 g; Saturated fat: 10 g; Cholesterol: 130 mg; Sodium: 346 mg; Potassium: 52 mg; Fiber: 1 g; Sugar: 1 g; Vitamin A: 5IU; Calcium: 232 mg; Iron: 1 mg

Keto Roast Beef Onion Bun Chaffle with Arby's Horsey Sauce

Serving: 2 Cook time: 10 min

INGREDIENTS

- Horseradish Sauce

- 1/2 cup mayonnaise

- 2 tsp keto sugar

- 2 tbsp horseradish from a container

- salt to taste

- Onion Bun Chaffle

- 1/2 cup ground mozzarella cheddar

- 1 tbsp minced onion

- salt to taste

- 4 ounces shop cook meat or cold extra dish hamburger

TRAVEL DIRECTIONS

1. Make the Horseradish Sauce early so the flavors can create

2. Join the mayonnaise, sugar, horseradish and salt in a bowl and put to the side in the cooler until prepared to make the Chaffles

3. Plug in the small waffle creator to preheat

4. In a little bowl, beat the egg, ground cheddar, minced onion and salt together.

5. When the waffle producer has heated up, pour a large portion of the player (around 1/4 cup) onto the creator and close the cover for 4 minutes.

6. Eliminate the Chaffle and permit to cool on a rack

7. Rehash with outstanding player.

8. Collect the sandwich by putting the dish meat on one chaffle, top with 1-2 tbsp of Horsey Sauce and top that with the other onion bun chaffle.

Sweet Chaffles Recipes

Lemon Curd Chaffles

Servings: 1 Cooking time: 5 minutes

INGREDIENTS

- 3 large eggs
- 4 oz cream cheese, softened
- 1 tablespoon low-carbohydrate sweetener
- 1 teaspoon of vanilla extract
- ¾ cup of mozzarella cheese, shredded
- 3 tablespoons of coconut flour
- 1 tsp baking powder
- ⅓ teaspoon of salt
- For the lemon curd:
- ½ - 1 cup of water
- 5 egg yolks
- ½ cup of lemon juice
- ½ cup of powdered sweetener
- 2 tablespoons of fresh lemon zest
- 1 teaspoon of vanilla extract
- Pinch of salt

- 8 tablespoons of cold butter, cubed

TRAVEL DIRECTIONS

1. Pour water into a saucepan and heat over medium heat until it boils gently. Start with ½ cup and add more if necessary.
2. Beat yolks, lemon juice, lemon zest, sweetener powder, vanilla, and salt in a medium heatproof bowl. Let it set for 5-6 minutes.
3. Place the bowl on the pan and heat. The bowl should not touch water.
4. Beat the mixture for 8-10 minutes, or until it starts to thicken.
5. Add butter cubes and beat for 7 minutes, until it thickens.
6. Remove from heat when lightly coated with the back of a spoon.
7. Cool until cool so it can thicken further.
8. Turn on the waffle iron to heat it up and coat it with cooking spray.
9. Add baking powder, coconut flour and salt in a small bowl. Mix well and set aside.
10. Add eggs, cream cheese, sweetener and vanilla in a separate bowl. Beat with a hand beater until frothy.
11. Add mozzar ella to the egg mixture and beat again.
12. Add dry and mix until well blended.
13. Add the batter to the waffle iron and cook for 3-4 minutes.
14. Before serving, spoon onto a plate and cover with lemon curd.

Nutritional Information: Carbohydrates: 6 g; Fat: 24 g; Protein: g Calories - 302

Peanut Butter Chaffles

Servings: 2 Cooking time: 8 minutes

INGREDIENTS

- 1 organic egg, beaten
- ½ cup of mozzarella cheese, shredded
- 3 tablespoons of granular erythritol
- 2 tablespoons of peanut butter

TRAVEL DIRECTIONS

1. Preheat a mini waffle iron and then grease it.
2. Place all in a medium bowl and mix with a fork until well blended.
3. Put half of the mixture in the preheated wafer and bake for about 4 minutes until golden brown.
4. Repeat with the remaining mixture.
5. Serve warm.

Nutritional Information:

- Calories: 145 Net Carbs: 2 Fat: 11.5g Saturated Fat: 3.1g
  Carbohydrates: 3.6g Dietary Fiber: 1g Sugar: 1.7g Protein: 8.8g

Choco late Chips Chaffles

Servings: 2 Cooking time: 8 minutes

INGREDIENTS

- 1 large organic egg
- 1 teaspoon of coconut flour
- 1 teaspoon of Erythritol
- ½ teaspoon of organic vanilla extract
- ½ cup of mozzarella cheese, finely chopped
- 2 tablespoons of 70% dark chocolate chips

TRAVEL DIRECTIONS

1. Preheat a mini waffle iron and then grease it.
2. Place the egg, coconut flour, sweetener and vanilla extract in a bowl and beat until well blended.
3. Add the cheese and stir to combine.
4. Place half of the mixture in the preheated waffle iron and cover with half of the chocolate chips.
5. Place a small egg mixture over each chocolate chip.
6. Cook for about 3-4 minutes or until golden brown.
7. Repeat with the remaining mixture and chocolate chips.
8. Serve warm.

Nutritional Information

- Calories: 164 Net Carbs: 2 Fat: 11.9g Saturated Dietary Fiber: 2.5g Sugar: 0.3g Protein: 7.3g

Basic Keto Chaffles

Servings: 2 Cooking time: 5 minutes

INGREDIENTS

- 1 egg
- ½ cup of grated Cheddar cheese

TRAVEL DIRECTIONS

1. Turn on the waffle iron to heat it up and coat it with cooking spray.
2. Beat the egg in a bowl until well beaten.
3. Add cheese to the egg and stir well to combine.
4. Pour ½ batter into the waffle iron and close the top. Cook for 3-5 minutes.
5. Transfer the chaffle to a plate and set aside for 2-3 minutes to get crispy.
6. Repeat for the remaining batter.

Nutritional Information: Carbohydrates: 1 g; Fat: 12 g; Protein: 9 g; Calories: 150

Red Velvet Chaffles

Servings: 2 Cooking time: 8 minutes

INGREDIENTS

- 2 tablespoons of cocoa powder
- 2 tablespoons of erythritol
- 1 organic egg, beaten
- 2 drops of super red food coloring
- ¼ teaspoon of organic baking powder
- 1 tablespoon of heavy whipping cream

TRAVEL DIRECTIONS

1. Preheat a mini waffle iron and then grease it.
2. Place all in a medium bowl and mix with a fork until well blended.
3. Put half of the mixture in the preheated waffle iron and cook for about 4 minutes.
4. Repeat with the remaining mixture.
5. Serve warm.

Nutritional information:

- Calories 70 Net carbohydrates 1.7 g Total fat g Saturated fat 3 g Cholesterol 92 mg Sodium 34 mg Total carbohydrates 3.2 g Fiber 1.5 g Sugar 0.2 g Protein 3.9 g

Mayonnaise Chaffles

Servings: 2 Cooking time: 10 minutes

INGREDIENTS

- 1 large organic egg, beaten 1 tablespoon mayonnaise
- 2 tablespoons of almond flour
- 1/8 teaspoon of organic baking powder
- 1 teaspoon of water 2-4 drops of liquid stevia

TRAVEL DIRECTIONS

1. Preheat a mini waffle iron and then grease it.
2. Place all in a medium bowl and mix with a fork until well blended. Place half of the mixture in a preheated waffle iron and cook for about 4-5 minutes.
3. Repeat with the remaining mixture.
4. Serve warm.

Nutritional information:

- Calories 110 Net carbohydrates 2.6 g Total fat 8.7 g Saturated fat 1.4 g Cholesterol 9 mg Sodium 88 g Total carbohydrates 3.4 g Fiber 0.8 g Sugar 0.9 g Protein 3.2 g

Chocolate Peanut Butter Chaffle

Servings: 2 Cooking time: 10 minutes

INGREDIENTS

- ½ cup of grated mozzarella cheese
- 1 tablespoon of cocoa powder
- 2 tablespoons of powdered sweetener
- 2 tablespoons of peanut butter
- ½ teaspoon vanilla
- 1 egg
- 2 tablespoons of ground peanuts
- 2 tablespoons of whipped cream
- ¼ cup of sugar-free chocolate syrup

TRAVEL DIRECTIONS

1. Combine mozzarella, egg, vanilla, peanut butter, cocoa powder, and sweetener in a bowl.
2. Add peanuts and mix well.
3. Turn on the waffle iron and coat it with cooking spray.
4. Pour half of the batter into the waffle iron and cook for minutes, then place on a plate.
5. Top with whipped cream, peanuts, and sugar-free chocolate syrup.

Nutritional Information:

- Carbohydrates: g; Fat: 17 g; Protein: 15 g; Calories: 236

Walnut Pumpkin Chaffles

Servings: 2 Cooking time: 10 minutes

INGREDIENTS

- 1 organic egg, beaten
- ½ cup of mozzarella cheese, shredded
- 2 tablespoons of almond flour
- 1 tablespoon sugar-free pumpkin puree
- 1 teaspoon of Erythritol
- ¼ teaspoon of cinnamon powder
- 2 tablespoons of walnuts, toasted and chopped

TRAVEL DIRECTIONS

1. Preheat a mini waffle iron and then grease it.
2. Place all except the walnuts in a bowl and beat until well blended.
3. Fold in the walnuts.
4. Place half of the mixture in the preheated waffle iron and bake for about 5 minutes or until golden brown.
5. Repeat with the remaining mixture.
6. Serve warm.

Nutritional Information:

- Calories: 148 Net Carbs: 1.6g Fat: 11.8g Saturated Fat: 2g Carbohydrates: 3.3g Dietary Fiber: 1. Sugar: 0.8g Protein: 6.7g

Simple Mozzarella Chaffles

Servings: 2 Cooking time: 8 minutes

INGREDIENTS

- ½ cup of mozzarella cheese, cut into pieces
- 1 large organic egg
- 2 tablespoons of blanched almond flour
- ¼ teaspoon of organic baking powder
- 2–3 drops of liquid stevia

TRAVEL DIRECTIONS

1. Preheat a mini waffle iron and then grease it.
2. Place all in a medium bowl and mix with a fork until well blended. Place half of the mixture in a preheated waffle iron and cook for about 3-4 minutes.
3. Repeat with the remaining mixture.
4. Serve warm.

Nutritional information:

- Calories 98 Net carbohydrates 1.4 g Total fat 7.1 g Saturated fat 1.8 g Cholesterol 97 mg Sodium 81 mg Total carbohydrates 2.2 g Fiber 0.8 g Sugar 0.2 g Protein 6.7 g

Savory Chaffles Recipes

Monte Cristo Chaffle Crepes

Serving: 3 Cook time: 15 min

INGREDIENTS

- 1 T almond flour
- 1/4 tsp vanilla extract
- 1/2 T Swerve Confectioners
- 1 T cream cheese, softened
- 1 tsp heavy cream
- Cinnamon

TRAVEL DIRECTIONS

Let batter rest for 5 minutes.

Pour it 1 1/2 Tablespoons of batter in preheated dash griddle.

Cook 30 seconds.

Flip with tongs and cook a few more seconds.

Put 1 slice of cheese, 1 slice of ham and 1 slice of turkey on each crepe.

If desired, microwave for a few seconds to melt the cheese.

Roll the crepes with the filling on the inside.

Present the filled crepes sprinkled with Swerve Confectioners and drizzled with low carb raspberry jam.

Nutritional Information:

- Amount Per Serving
- Calories   60
- % Daily Value*
- Total Fat 4g   5%
- Cholesterol 67.8mg   23%
- Sodium 39.2mg   2%
- Total Carbohydrate 2.1g   1%
- Dietary Fiber 0.5g   2%
- Sugars 0.9g
- Protein 2.8g   6%
- Vitamin A 45.1µg   5%
- Vitamin C 0mg   0%

Dairy Free Chaffle

Serving: 3 Cook time: 10 min

INGREDIENTS

- large egg
- 1 TB coconut cream *see notes
- TB almond butter
- 1/4 tsp xanthan gum
- 1/4 tsp baking powder

TRAVEL DIRECTIONS

1. Firstly, Whisk egg in a bowl or Pyrex measuring cup. Add the coconut cream and almond butter and whisk until smooth.
2. Mix the xanthan gum, baking powder and salt in a small bowl. Mix to ensure that the xanthan gum is distributed. Then whisk these dry into your batter.
3. Then Divide the batter between two Dash Mini waffle makers and cook for 3 minutes.
4. Remove to a cooling rack for at least 2-3 minutes before serving.

Nutritional Information:

- Calories per serving: 120 Kcal ; Fat: 10g ; Carbohydrates: 2g ; Protein: 12

Cream Cheese Coconut Flour Chaffles Two Ways (Sweet & Savory)

Serving: 2 Cook time: 10 min

INGREDIENTS

- 4 oz cream cheese softened
- 4 large eggs
- 4 tbsp coconut flour
- 1 tsp baking powder
- 1 tbsp melted butter
- 2 tsp vanilla
- 1 tbsp keto sugar
- 1 tbsp sugar-free cocoa powder

TRAVEL DIRECTIONS

1. Preheat waffle iron according to instructions
2. Mix eggs, cream cheese, and melted butter well, using a whisk or personal blender
3. Add all other to mixture and combine well
4. Add half of this batter to heated waffle iron, if using full-size iron. Use a smaller amount if using a mini waffle maker
5. Serve and appreciate

Easy Keto Bacon Chaffles

Servings: 2 Cook time: 10 min

INGREDIENTS

- 2 eggs
- ½ cup cheddar cheese
- ½ cup mozzarella cheese
- ¼ tsp baking powder
- ½ tbsp almond flour
- tbsp butter, for waffle iron

TRAVEL DIRECTIONS

1. Firstly, add the eggs, cheddar, mozzarella, baking powder, and almond flour to a blender and pulse 10 times so the cheese is still chunky.
2. Then Add 1/4 cup of the bacon and 2 tbsp of green onions or chives. Pulse 2-3 times to combine.
3. Add the butter in iron waffle maker and make sure it's coated entirely. Add half of the batter and cook for 3 minutes or until golden brown. Repeat with the rest of the batter. Makes 2 large chaffles.
4. Add your favorite toppings and appreciate.

Nutritional Information:

- Fat 38g58%
- Saturated Fat 19g119%
- Cholesterol 250mg83%
- Sodium 714mg31%
- Potassium 168mg5%
- Carbohydrates 3g1%
- Fiber 1g4%
- Sugar 1g1%
- Protein 23g46%

Broccoli and Cheese Chaffle Recipe

Servings: 2 Cook time: 8 min

INGREDIENTS

- 1/2 cup cheddar cheese
- 1/4 cup fresh chopped broccoli
- egg
- 1/4 teaspoon garlic powder
- 1 tablespoon almond flour

TRAVEL DIRECTIONS

1. Then in a bowl mix almond flour, cheddar cheese, egg and garlic powder. I find it easiest to mix everything using a fork.
2. Then Add half the Broccoli and Cheese Chaffle batter to the Dish Mini waffle maker at a time. Cook chaffle batter in the waffle maker for 4 minutes.
3. Let each chaffle sit for 1-2 minutes on a plate to firm up. Enjoy

Nutritional Information:

- Serving: 1g | Calories: 170kcal | Carbohydrates: 2g | Protein: 11g | Fat: 13g | Saturated Fat: 7g | Cholesterol: 112mg | Sodium: 211mg | Potassium: 94mg | Fiber: 1g | Sugar: 1g | Vitamin A: 473IU | Vitamin C: 10mg | Calcium:

Taco Chaffle Recipe

Servings: 1 Cook time; 8 min

INGREDIENTS
- egg white
- 1/4 cup Monterey jack cheddar, shredded (pressed firmly)
- 1/4 cup sharp cheddar, shredded (stuffed firmly)
- 3/4 tsp water
- 1 tsp coconut flour
- 1/4 tsp preparing powder
- 1/8 tsp stew powder
- spot of salt

TRAVEL DIRECTIONS
1. Plug the Dash Mini Waffle Maker in the divider and oil delicately once it is hot.
2. Consolidate the entirety of the in a bowl and mix to join.
3. Spoon out 1/2 of the hitter on the waffle creator and close cover. Set a clock for 4 minutes and don't lift the cover until the cooking time is finished. In the event that you do, it will resemble the taco chaffle shell

isn't setting up as expected, yet it will. You need to allow it to cook the whole 4 minutes prior to lifting the top.

4. Eliminate the taco chaffle shell from the waffle iron and put in a safe spot. Rehash similar strides above with the remainder of the chaffle hitter.

5. Turn over a biscuit skillet and set the taco chaffle shells between the cups to shape a taco shell. Permit to set for a couple of moments.

6. Eliminate and present with the Very Best Taco Meat or your number one formula.

7. Enjoy this tasty keto firm taco chaffle shell with your number one fixings.

Nutritional Information:

- Serving: 2g | Calories: 258kcal | Carbohydrates: 4g | Protein: 18g | Fat: 19g | Fiber: 2g | Sugar: 1g

Lunch Chaffle Recipes

Grill Pork Chaffle Sandwich

Servings: 2 Cooking time: 15 minutes

INGREDIENTS

- 1/2 cup mozzarella, shredded
- 1 egg
- I squeeze garlic powder
- PORK PATTY
- 1/2 cup pork, cut in minutes
- 1 tbsp. green onion, diced
- 1/2 teaspoon of Italian seasoning
- Save leaves

TRAVEL DIRECTIONS

1. Preheat and grease the square waffle iron
2. Combine egg, cheese and garlic powder in a small mixing bowl.
3. Pour the batter into a preheated waffle iron and close the lid.
4. Make 2 chaffles with this whipped cream.
5. Cook chaffles for about 2-3 minutes until tender.
6. Meanwhile, mix the of the pork patties in a bowl and make 1 large burger.
7. Grill the pork patties in a preheated grill for about 3-4 minutes per side until cooked through.

8. Arrange the pork patties between two chaffles with salad leaves. Cut the sandwich to make a triangular sandwich.
9. To enjoy!

Nutritional Information:
- Per Servings: Protein: 48% 85 kcal Fat: 48% 86 kcal Carbohydrates: 4% 7 kcal

Grill Steak and Chaffle

Servings: 1 Cooking time: 10 minutes

INGREDIENTS

- 1 beefsteak rib eye
- 1 tsp salt
- 1 tsp pepper
- 1 tbsp. lime juice
- 1 tsp garlic

TRAVEL DIRECTIONS

1. Prep your grill for direct heat.
2. Mix all the spices together and rub the steak evenly.
3. Place the beef on the grill rack over medium heat.
4. Cover and cook the steak for about 6 to 8 minutes. Flip and cook for another 5 minutes until cooked through.
5. Serve with Keto Simple Chaffle and enjoy!

Nutritional Information:

- Per Servings: Protein: 51% 274 kcal Fat: 45% 243 kcal Carbohydrates: 4% 22 kcal

Chaffle & Chicken Lunch Plate

Servings: 1 Cooking time: 15 minutes

INGREDIENTS

- 1 large egg
- 1/2 cup farmer's cheese, shredded
- 1 pinch of salt
- To serve
- 1 chicken leg
- salt
- pepper
- 1 tsp. garlic, in minutes
- 1 egg
- I teaspoon of avocado oil

TRAVEL DIRECTIONS

1. Heat your square waffle iron and grease with cooking spray.
2. Pour Chaffle batter into the pan and cook for about 3 minutes.
3. Meanwhile, heat oil in a pan over medium heat.
4. Once the oil is hot, add chicken thighs and garlants and cook for about 5 minutes. Flip and cook for another 3-4 minutes.
5. Season with salt and pepper and mix well.
6. Transfer the caged thigh to the plate.
7. Fry the egg in the same pan for about 1-2 minutes of your choice.

8. When the chaffles are cooked, serve with fried egg and chicken thigh.
9. To enjoy!

Nutritional Information:

- Protein: 31% 138 kcal Fat: 66% 292 kcal Carbohydrates: 2% kcal

Chaffle Egg Sandwich

Servings: 2 Cooking time: 10 minutes

INGREDIENTS

- 2 minutes I keto chaffle
- 2 slices of cheddar cheese
- 1 egg simple omelette

TRAVEL DIRECTIONS

1. Prepare your oven for 4000 F.
2. Divide the egg omelette and cheese slice between chaffles.
3. Bake in the preheated oven for about 4-5 minutes until the cheese has melted.
4. Once the cheese has melted, remove it from the oven.
5. Serve and enjoy!

Nutritional Information:

- Per Servings: Protein: 29% 144 kcal Fat: 337% kcal Carbohydrates: 3% 14 kcal

Chicken Zinger Chaffle

Servings: 2 Cooking time: 15 minutes

INGREDIENTS

- 1 chicken fillet, cut into 2 pieces
- 1/2 cup of coconut flour
- 1/4 cup finely grated Parmesan cheese
- 1 tsp. Bell pepper
- 1/2 tsp. garlic powder
- 1/2 tsp. onion powder
- 1 tsp. salt pepper
- 1 egg beaten
- Avocado oil for frying
- Lettuce leaves
- Barbecue sauce
- CHAFFLE
- 4 oz. cheese
- 2 whole eggs
- 2 ounces. almond flour
- 1/4 cup of almond flour
- 1 tsp baking powder

TRAVEL DIRECTIONS

1. Mix the chaffle in a bowl.
2. Pour the chaffle batter into the preheated, greased square chaffle maker.

3. Cook chaffles for about 2 minutes until tender.
4. Make square chaffles from this batter.
5. Meanwhile, mix coconut flour, parmesan, paprika, garlic powder, onion powder, salt and pepper in a bowl.
6. Dip chicken in coconut flour mixture first and then in beaten egg.
7. Heat avocado oil in a skillet and fry chicken on both sides. until light brown and cooked through
8. Place the chicken zinger between two chaffles with lettuce and barbecue sauce.
9. To enjoy!

Nutritional Information:
- Per Servings: Protein: 30% 219 kcal Fat: 60% 435 kcal Carbohydrates: 9% 66 kcal

Double Chicken Chaffles

Servings: 2 Cooking time: 5 minutes

INGREDIENTS

- 1/2 cup cook shredded chicken
- 1/4 cup of cheddar cheese
- 1/8 cup of parmesan cheese
- 1 egg
- 1 tsp. Italian spices
- 1/8 tsp. garlic powder
- 1 tsp. cream cheese

TRAVEL DIRECTIONS

1. Preheat the Belgian waffle iron.
2. Combine the chaffle in a bowl and mix them together.
3. Sprinkle 1 tbsp. of cheese in a waffle iron and pour the whipped cream batter.
4. Pour 1 tbsp. of cheese over batter and close the lid.
5. Cook chaffles for about 4 to minutes.
6. Serve with a chicken zinger and enjoy the double chicken flavor.

Nutritional Information:

- Per Servings: Protein: 30% 60 kcal Fat: 65% 129 kcal
  Carbohydrates: 5% 9 kcal

Simple Chaffle Recipes

Hot Ham Roll Ups with Cheese

Servings: 12 Cook time: 30 min

INGREDIENTS

- Smoked Deli Ham 12 pieces
- 12 Mozzarella Cheese Sticks
- tablespoon of butter

TRAVEL DIRECTIONS

1. Firstly, heat 1 tablespoon of butter in a non-stick skillet.
2. Then wrap a piece of ham around a mozzarella cheese stick. Reliant on how large your ham slices are, you may need to cut the cheese sticks in half.
3. Fry the mozzarella stick wrapped in ham in the butter until browned on all sides.
4. Serve and appreciate!

Nutritional Information:

- Calories: 156kcal | Carbohydrates: 1g | Protein: 12g | Fat: 12g | Saturated Fat: 6g | Cholesterol: 35mg | Sodium: 561mg | Potassium: 80mg | Sugar: 1g | Vitamin A: 29IU | Calcium: 22mg | Iron: 1mg

Easy Keto Chaffle Recipe (Higlhly Popular Recipe)

Servings1: Cook time: 8 min

INGREDIENTS
- egg (or simply an egg white for a crispier chaffle)
- 1/2 cup cheddar, destroyed

TRAVEL DIRECTIONS
1. Turn waffle producer on or plug it in with the goal that it warms and oil the two sides.
2. In a little bowl, break an egg at that point add the 1/2 cup cheddar and mix to consolidate.
3. For a crispier chaffle utilize only the egg white rather than the whole egg.
4. Pour 1/2 of the hitter in the waffle producer and close the top.
5. Cook for 3-4 minutes or until it arrives at wanted doneness.
6. Cautiously eliminate from waffle creator and put in a safe spot for 2-3 minutes to give it an opportunity to fresh.
7. Adhere to the guidelines again to make the second chaffle.
8. This formula for a customary chaffle makes phenomenal sandwiches.

Nutrition Information:
- Serving: 1g | Calories: 291kcal | Carbohydrates: 1g | Protein: 20g | Fat: 23g | Saturated Fat: 13g | Cholesterol: 223mg | Sodium: 413mg | Potassium: 116mg | Sugar: 1g | Vitamin A: 804IU | Calcium: 432mg | Iron: 1mg

Easy Keto Pizza Chaffles

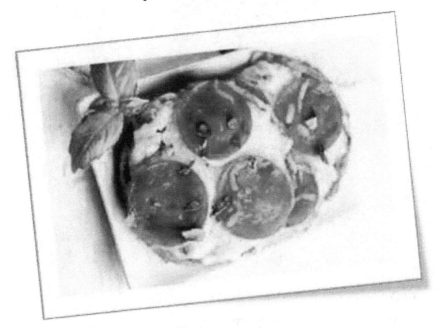

Servings:2 Cook time: 6 min

INGREDIENTS

- large egg
- ½ teaspoon Italian seasoning
- ½ cup plus 2 teaspoons shredded part-skim low-moisture mozzarella cheese, plus more for the topping
- tablespoons Rao's homemade pizza sauce
- Sliced pepperoni or any of your favorite toppings, optional

TRAVEL DIRECTIONS

1. Firstly, PREHEAT a mini waffle maker
2. In a small bowl, whisk together the egg and Italian seasoning. Add the ½ cup mozzarella cheese and mix.
3. teaspoon mozzarella into the waffle maker and let it cook for 30 seconds. Add half the batter and cook until golden brown and crispy, about 4 minutes. Transfer the chaffle to a microwave-safe plate.
4. Then Repeat with the remaining 1 teaspoon mozzarella and batter.
5. TOP each chaffle with 1 tablespoon pizza sauce, additional shredded
6. mozzarella, and pepperoni, if using. Heat in the microwave for about 20 seconds and present immediately

Nutritional Information:

- YIELD: 2 SERVING SIZE: 1 Pizza
- Amount Per Serving: CALORIES: 106TOTAL FAT: 6.7gCARBOHYDRATES: 2.7gNET CARBOHYDRATES: 2.4gFIBER: .3gPROTEIN: 8.5g

Wonder Bread Chaffles (soft & delish)

Servings: 2 Cook time: 10 min

INGREDIENTS

- large egg
- tbsp almond flour
- 1 tbsp mayonnaise
- 1/4 tsp baking powder
- 1 tsp water

TRAVEL DIRECTIONS

1. Firstly, preheat your mini waffle maker.
2. Whisk together the egg in a small bowl until well beaten.
3. Add the almond flour, mayo, baking powder and water; mix well.
4. Then Spray your waffle maker with non-stick spray and pour half of your batter in. Close the lid and allow to cook it for about 3 minutes or until the timer or light goes off. Repeat for second waffle.

Nutritional Information:

- Saturated Fat: 4g | Cholesterol: 104mg | Sodium: 207mg | Potassium: 52mg | Sugar: 1g | Vitamin A: 308IU | Calcium: 154mg | Iron: 1mg

Sourdough Chaffles

Serving: 2 Chaffles Cook time: 10 min

INGREDIENTS

- 2 egg whites
- 1/2 cup mozzarella
- 2 tbsp almond flour
- 2 tbsp sour cream

TRAVEL DIRECTIONS

1. Firstly, use a fork or whisk and whip the egg whites until frothy.
2. Then Add the remaining and combine well.
3. Spray both sides of the chaffle maker with cooking spray or oil. This is optional but will help keep them from sticking.
4. Pour half the batter into a pre-heated chaffle maker and close the lid
5. Cook for about 4-5 minutes or until the chaffle is golden brown and releases easily.
6. Repeat and appreciate!

Nutritional Information:

- Serving: 2chaffles | Calories: 331kcal | Carbohydrates: 6g | Protein: 23g | Fat: 24g | Saturated Fat: 10g | Polyunsaturated Fat: 12g | Cholesterol: 58mg | Sodium: 468mg | Fiber: 2g | Sugar: 2g | Net Carbohydrates: 4g

Cheddar Chive Chaffles

Cook time: 3 min Servings: 2

INGREDIENTS

- large egg
- ½ cup cheddar cheese finely shredded
- ¼ cup super fine almond flour
- 1 teaspoon chives finely chopped

TRAVEL DIRECTIONS

1. Firstly, preheat the waffle maker.
2. Then place egg in a small mixing bowl and lightly whisk.
3. Now Add in cheddar cheese, almond flour and chives. Combine together until the batter is combined. Stir in the salt.
4. Spray waffle iron with coconut oil and Scoop the batter onto the waffle iron and cook for 3 to 4 minutes or until chaffle is golden brown and cooked through.
5. Remove chaffle from the waffle iron and place on a cooling rack. Cool the chaffle completely before presenting

Nutritional Information:

- Amount Per Serving (2 waffles)
- Calories 277Calories from Fat 198
- % Daily Value*

- Fat 22g34%
- Saturated Fat 9g56%
- Trans Fat 0g
- Polyunsaturated Fat 1g
- Monounsaturated Fat 6g
- Cholesterol 231mg77%
- Sodium 341mg15%
- Potassium 109mg3%
- Carbohydrates 3g

Crispy Keto Chaffle

Servings: 2 Cook time: 6 min

INGREDIENTS

- Egg
- 1/2 Cup Shredded Cheese

TRAVEL DIRECTIONS

1. Firstly, Plug-in Dash Mini Waffle Maker to pre-heat.
2. In a small mixing bowl, beat egg.
3. Place about 1/8 cup Shredded Cheese on to the Dash Mini Waffle Maker, followed by ~1/2 of the egg paste and another 1/8 cup of Shredded Mozzarella Cheese on top. Close lid and cook for 3 - 4 minutes. Repeat for as many waffles you are making.
4. Now let the chaffle cool for a few minutes before assembling your favorite sandwich.

Nutritional Information:

- Calories: 115kcal | Carbohydrates: 1g | Protein: 9g | Fat: 8g | Saturated Fat: 4g | Cholesterol: 104mg | Sodium: 207mg | Potassium: 52mg | Sugar: 1g | Vitamin A: 308IU | Calcium: 154mg | Iron: 1mg

Keto Chaffle Recipes Variations

Chaffle cake

Servings: 2 Cooking time: 8 minutes

INGREDIENTS

- Chocolate Chaffle Cake
- 2 tablespoons of cocoa powder
- 2 tablespoons Swerve Granulated Sweetener
- 1 egg
- 1 tablespoon of heavy whipping cream
- 1 tablespoon of almond flour
- 1/4 teaspoon baking powder
- 1/2 teaspoon vanilla extract
- Cream cheese icing:
- 2 tablespoons of cream cheese
- 2 teaspoons swerve confectioners
- 1/8 teaspoon vanilla extract

- 1 teaspoon of whipped cream

TRAVEL DIRECTIONS
1. How to make chocolate cake:
2. In a small bowl, beat cocoa powder, swerve, almond flour, and baking powder together.
3. Add the vanilla extract and heavy whipping cream and mix well.
4. Add the egg and mix well. Make sure to scrape the sides of the bowl to mix all the well.
5. Let stand for 3-4 minutes while the mini waffle iron heats up.
6. Add half of the waffle mixture to the waffle iron and cook for 4 minutes. Then cook the second wafer. Make your icing while the second chocolate keto wafer is cooking.
7. How To Make Cream Cheese Frosting?
8. In a small microwave-safe bowl, add 2 tablespoons of cream cheese. Microwave the cream cheese for seconds to soften the cream cheese.
9. Add heavy whipping cream and vanilla extract and use a small hand mixer to mix well.
10. Then add the confectioners and use the hand mixer to soak up the icing and make it fluffy.
11. Keto Chocolate Chaffle c ake assemblies:
12. Put a chocolate chip cake on a plate, cover with a layer of icing. You can spread it out with a knife or use a piping bag and spray the icing.
13. Place the second chocolate chip cake on top of the icing and spread or spray the rest of the froangel on top.

Nutritional Information:
- (per serving): Calories: 151 kcal; Carbohydrates: 5 g; Protein: 6 g; Fat: 13 g; Saturated fat: 6 g; Cholesterol: 111 mg; Sodium: 83 mg; Potassium: 190 mg; Fiber: 2 g; Sugar: 1 g; Vitamin A: 461IU; Calcium: 67 mg; Iron: 1 mg

Keto Chaffle Breakfast sandwich

Servings: 1 Cooking time: 6 minutes

INGREDIENTS

- 1 egg
- 1/2 cup Monterey Jack Cheese
- 1 tablespoon of almond flour
- 2 tablespoons of butter

TRAVEL DIRECTIONS

1. In a small bowl, combine the egg, almond flour, and Monterey Jack Cheese.
2. Pour half of the batter into your mini waffle iron and cook for 3-4 minutes. Then boil the rest of the batter to make a second chaffle.
3. In a small saucepan, melt 2 tablespoons of butter. Add the chaffles and fry for 2 minutes on each side. Pressure sings as they cook lightly on top so they get crispy better.
4. Remove from pan and let stand for 2 minutes.

Nutritional Information:

- (per serving): Calories: 4 kcal; Carbohydrates: 2 g; Protein: 21 g; Fat: 47 g; Saturated fat: 27 g; Cholesterol: 274 mg; Sodium: 565 mg; Potassium: 106 mg; Fiber: 1 g; Sugar: 1 g; Vitamin A: 1372IU; Calcium: 461 mg; Iron: 1 mg

Cinnamon Roll Keto Chaffles

Servings: 3 Cooking time: 10 minutes

INGREDIENTS

- Cinnamon Roll Chaffle
- 1/2 cup of mozzarella cheese
- 1 tablespoon of almond flour
- 1/4 teaspoon baking powder
- 1 egg
- 1 teaspoon of cinnamon
- 1 teaspoon granulated swerve
- Cinnamon bun swirl
- 1 tbsp butter
- 1 teaspoon of cinnamon
- 2 teaspoons of confectioners give way
- Keto Cinnamon Roll Frosting
- 1 tablespoon of butter
- 1 tablespoon of cream cheese
- 1/4 teaspoon vanilla extract
- 2 teaspoons of alternate confectioners

TRAVEL DIRECTIONS

1. Plug in your Mini Dash Waffle Maker and let it heat up.
2. In a small bowl, combine the mozzarella cheese, almond flour, baking powder, egg, 1 teaspoon cinnamon and 1 teaspoon granulate and set aside.
3. In another small bowl, add a tablespoon of butter, 1 teaspoon of cinnamon, and 2 teaspoons of confectioner's sweetener.
4. Microwave for 15 seconds and mix well.
5. Spray the waffle iron with nonstick cooking spray and add 1/3 of the batter to your waffle iron. Stir in 1/3 of the cinnamon, whisk and butter mixture. Close the waffle iron and cook for 3-4 minutes.
6. When the first cinnamon roll is done, make the second and then the third.
7. While the third chaffle is cooking, place 1 tablespoon of butter and 1 tablespoon of cream cheese in a small bowl. Heat in the microwave for 10-15 seconds. Start at 10 and if the cream cheese is not soft enough to mix with the butter, heat for an additional 5 seconds.
8. Add the vanilla extract and confectioners' sweetener to the butter and cream cheese and mix well with a whisk.
9. Drizzle keto cream cheese frosting over the chaffle.

Nutritional Information:

- (per serving): Calories: 180 kcal; Carbohydrates: 3 g; Protein: 7 g; Fat: 16 g; Saturated fat: 9 g; Cholesterol: 95 mg; Sodium: 221 mg; Potassium: 77 mg; Fiber: 1 g; Sugar: 1 g; Vitamin A: 505 IU; Calcium: 148 mg; Iron: 1 mg

Vegetarian Chaffle Recipes

Mushroom and Almond Chaffle

Servings: 4 Cooking time: 15 minutes

INGREDIENTS

- Seizure
- 4 eggs
- 2 cups of grated mozzarella cheese
- 1 cup of finely chopped zucchini
- 3 tablespoons of chopped almonds
- 2 teaspoons of baking powder
- Salt and pepper to taste
- 1 teaspoon of dried basil
- 1 teaspoon chili flakes
- Others
- 2 tablespoons of cooking spray to brush the waffle iron

TRAVEL DIRECTIONS

1. Preheat the waffle iron.
2. Add the eggs, grated mozzarella, mushrooms, almonds, baking powder, salt and pepper, dried basil, and chili flakes to a bowl.
3. Mix with a fork.
4. Brush the heated waffle iron with cooking spray and add a few tablespoons of the batter.
5. Close the lid and cook for about 7 minutes, depending on your waffle iron.
6. Serve and enjoy.

Nutritional Information:

- Calories 196, Fat 16g, Carbohydrates 4g, Sugar 1g, Protein 10.8g, Sodium 152mg

Spinach and Artichoke Chaffle

Servings: 4 Cooking time: 15 minutes

INGREDIENTS:

- Seizure
- 4 eggs
- 2 cups of grated provolone cheese
- 1 cup of cooked and diced spinach
- ½ cup diced artichoke hearts
- Salt and pepper to taste
- 2 tablespoons of coconut flour
- 2 teaspoons of baking powder
- Others
- 2 tablespoons of cooking spray to brush the waffle iron
- ¼ cup of cream cheese to serve

TRAVEL DIRECTIONS

1. Preheat the waffle iron.
2. Add the eggs, grated provolone cheese, spinach cubes, artichoke hearts, salt and pepper, coconut flour and baking powder to a bowl.
3. Mix with a fork.

4. Brush the heated waffle iron with cooking spray and add a few tablespoons of the batter.

5. Close the lid and cook for about 7 minutes, depending on your waffle iron.

6. Serve each chaffle with cream cheese.

Nutritional Information:

- Calories 42, Fat 32.8g, Carbohydrates 9.5g, Sugar 1.1g, Protein 25.7g, Sodium 722mg

Avocado Croque Madam Chaffle

Servings: 4 Cooking time: 15 minutes

INGREDIENTS

- Seizure
- 4 eggs
- 2 cups of grated mozzarella cheese
- 1 avocado, mashed
- Salt and pepper to taste
- 6 tablespoons of almond flour
- 2 teaspoons of baking powder
- 1 teaspoon of dried dill
- Others
- 2 tablespoons of cooking spray to brush the waffle iron
- 4 fried eggs
- 2 tablespoons of freshly chopped basil

TRAVEL DIRECTIONS

1. Preheat the waffle iron.
2. Add the eggs, grated mozzarella, avocado, salt and pepper, almond flour, baking powder and dried dill to a bowl.
3. Mix with a fork.

4. Brush the heated waffle iron with cooking spray and add a few tablespoons of the batter.

5. Close the lid and cook for about 7 minutes, depending on your waffle iron.

6. Serve each chaffle with a fried egg and freshly chopped basil on top.

Nutritional Information:

- Calories 393, Fat 32.1g, Carbohydrates 9.2g, Sugar 1.3g, Protein 18.8g, Sodium 245mg

Other Keto Chaffle Recipes

Keto Carnivore Diet Chaffle Benedict Recipe

Servings: 2 Cook time: 30 min

INGREDIENTS

- cup shredded cheddar mozzarella is ideal
- 4 eggs separated
- tablespoons lemon juice
- egg yolks
- 10 tablespoons salted spread
- 1 teaspoon salt
- ¼ cup apple juice vinegar
- 4-6 cuts Jones Braunschweiger Liverwurst cuts
- chopped parsley discretionary

DIRECTIONS

1. Preheat the waffle creator.
2. Heartbeat 2 eggs and shredded cheddar in the blender until all around joined.
3. Pour the hitter in the blender.

4. Cook the waffle for 3-4 minutes until brilliant brown and they effectively lift out of the machine.
5. Rehash until all the player is spent and saved the cooked waffles.
6. Put the lemon, egg yolks in the blender and blend until consolidated.
7. With the blender running on a low setting, extremely, gradually add the margarine to the egg yolk combination in a meager stream until totally spent.
8. Following a moment or two an emulsion begins to frame.
9. Make a point to keep the slim stream consistent and delayed to try not to break the hollandaise.
10. At the point when all the margarine is added, the hollandaise ought to be medium thickness and prepared to serve.
11. Put the sauce in a safe spot and move to poaching the eggs.
12. Fill a little pot ¾ of the path with water, add the salt and vinegar.
13. Spot it over medium heat and bring to a moving bubble.
14. Drop the eggs into the water and let them cook for 3-4 minutes.
15. Utilize an opened spoon to eliminate them and spot on a paper towel to eliminate overabundance dampness.
16. Utilize a skillet to heat up the braunschweiger for 1-2 minutes over medium heat to get it browned on the two sides.
17. Amass the dish putting the waffles on a plate, finished off with braunshweiger, poached eggs, hollandaise sauce and new spices, if using.
18. Serve and enjoy.

Keto Belgian Chaffles

Servings: 2 Cook time: 4 min

DIRECTIONS:

1. Plug in the waffle iron to preheat.
2. While it is heating up, break the eggs into a little bowl and rush to scramble. Then, add the shredded cheddar and blend to consolidate.
3. At the point when the waffle iron is prepared, empty the combination into the waffle iron. The hitter makes 2 Belgian-sized chaffles. Each waffle depression can be filled totally. This player will extend yet not however much ordinary waffle hitter.
4. Close the waffle iron cover and let cook for 4 minutes. When prepared, lift the top and puncture an edge of a chaffle with a fork to lift and eliminate.
5. 2 servings and each chaffle = 300 calories, 23 fat, 20 protein, 2.6 carbs

Nutritional information:
- Fat 5 g 22% Carbohydrates 12.6 g of 5% Sugars 4.5 g

BEST KETO TUNA MELT CHAFFLE RECIPE

Serving: 3 Cook time: 20 min

INGREDIENTS

- packet Tuna 2.6 oz with no water
- 1/2 cup mozzarella cheese
- 1 egg
- pinch salt

DIRECTIONS:

1. Firstly, preheat the mini waffle maker.
2. In a small bowl, add the egg and whip it up.
3. Now Add the tuna, cheese, and salt and mix well.
4. Then Add 1/2 the mixture to the waffle maker and cook it for a minimum of 4 minutes.
5. Remove it and cook the last tuna chaffle for another 4 minutes.

Nutritional Information:

- Calories 123, Total C 1.2g, Fiber 0.5g, Net C 0.7g, Sugar 0.5g, Fat 3.5g, Protein 20.8g

Keto Chaffle with Chicken – Amish Style

Servings: 2 Cook time: 10 min

INGREDIENTS

- Chaffle
- Egg (beaten)
- 1/2 cup cheddar (ground)
- 1 tablespoon Almond flour (whitened)
- 1/2 teaspoon Baking powder
- Chicken and Gravy
- 1/2 cup Chicken bosom (coarsley shredded)
- tablespoons Butter (unsalted, dissolved)
- tablespoons Almond flour (whitened)
- 1 cup Chicken stock (ensure gluten free on name)
- tablespoons Heavy cream
- 1/8 teaspoon Poultry preparing (ground)
- 1/8 teaspoon Salt
- 1/8 teaspoon Pepper
- 1 Scallion (cut)
- 1/2 teaspoon Xanthan gum

DIRECTIONS:

1. Chaffle
2. Splash small waffle producer with cooking shower at that point preheat until prepared.
3. Empty sufficient hitter into the focal point of the waffle producer and spread to fill the edges. On the off chance that you stuff the first utilize less each time so you stay away from spill over. Close the top and permit to cook for 3 1/2 minutes.
4. Eliminate the chaffle and permit to cool on a cooling rack – rehash the interaction for the second chaffle.
5. Chicken and Gravy
6. In an enormous pan, soften the spread over medium heat. Mix in the almond flour and whisk continually until smooth; cook for 2 minutes. Bit by bit race in chicken stock, hefty cream, poultry preparing, thickener, and salt and pepper. Cook until thickend (3 minutes).
7. Mix in chicken and permit to heat for 2 minutes. Keep warm.
8. Serve the waffles finished off with the chicken and sauce, Garnish with cut scallions. Serve hot. (For considerably crisper waffes you can toast them, prior to fixing. This is a smart thought for pre-made waffles).

NUTRITION

- Calories: 435kcal | Carbohydrates: 5g | Protein: 21g | Fat: 38g | Saturated Fat: 20g | Cholesterol: 197mg | Sodium: 984mg | Potassium: 399mg | Fiber: 1g | Sugar: 1g | Calcium: 339mg | Net Carbs: 4g

Potato Latke Waffles

Servings: 3 Cook time: 30 min

INGREDIENTS

- 1/2 White onion, diced or daintily cut
- 2 Eggs
- 1/2 cup Extra virgin olive oil
- tbsp salt
- 1/4 tsp Black pepper
- 1/2 tsp Smoked or sweet paprika

DIRECTIONS

1. Pre-heat waffle creator and splash with non-stick cooking shower
2. In a bowl, add the shredded potatoes, onion, eggs, salt, pepper, paprika and oil
3. Blend (using your hands is simpler - they're your best instrument) until completely blended
4. Spoon around 3/4 cup into waffle creator. You would prefer not to overstuff it on the grounds that the center will get firm however the sides will not, so ensure it's an even layer

5. You can utilize any sort of waffle producer - ordinary, Belgian, smaller than normal - and so on! Simply be patient and allowed them to concoct and fresh!

6. Present with an entire slew of fixings! In case you're making them dairy, add a storing spoonful of sharp cream or fruit purée. Making these meats? Add some chopped salami or pastrami and top with sriracha mayo!

Nutritional Information:

- Protein: 22% 40 kcal Fat: 66% 120 kcal Carbohydrates: 12% 22 kcal

Keto Chaffle Crab Roll

Servings: 2 Cook time: 6 min

INGREDIENTS

- 6 oz Crab Meat Canned Lump
- 2 tbsp Kewpie Mayo you can sub with American mayo yet will adjust taste
- tsp Lemon Juice
- 1 Egg
- 1/4 tsp Garlic Powder
- 1/4 tsp Bay Seasoning
- 1/2 Cup Shredded Mozzarella Cheese

INSTRUCTIONS:

1. Channel water from the canned crab and add crab into a little blending bowl, alongside Kewpie Mayo and lemon juice. Throw and set to the side.
2. Module Dash Mini Waffle Maker to pre-heat.
3. In a different little blending bowl, add egg, garlic powder, old inlet preparing, shredded Mozzarella cheddar and beat well.
4. Spot about ~1/2 of the egg combination on to the Dash Mini Waffle Maker. Close cover and cook for 3 - 4 minutes. Rehash for as numerous waffles you are making.
5. Scoop crab blend into the center of the cooked chaffle crease and enjoy!

NUTRITION INFORMATION:

- Calories: 290kcal | Carbohydrates: 1g | Protein: 25g | Fat: 19g | Saturated Fat: 6g | Cholesterol: 160mg | Sodium: 1018mg | Potassium: 225mg | Sugar: 1g | Vitamin A: 308IU | Vitamin C: 7mg | Calcium: 193mg | Iron: 1mg

CPSIA information can be obtained
at www.ICGtesting.com
Printed in the USA
BVHW060732010521
606210BV00007B/1745